D1450017

J940.5426 N521p
Nicholson, Dorinda...
Pearl Harbor warriors   APR 1 0 2003

MID-CONTINENT PUBLIC LIBRARY
Kearney Branch
100 S. Platte-Clay Way
Kearney, Mo. 64060

KE

WITHDRAWN
FROM THE RECORDS OF THE
MID-CONTINENT PUBLIC LIBRARY

Pearl Harbor WARRIORS

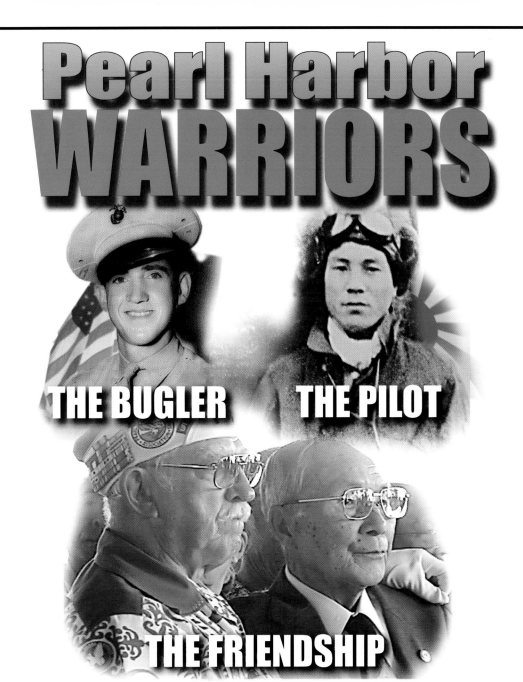

THE BUGLER

THE PILOT

THE FRIENDSHIP

by Dorinda Makanaonalani Nicholson
author of PEARL HARBOR CHILD

Illustrated by Larry Nicholson

MID-CONTINENT PUBLIC LIBRARY
Kearney Branch
100 S. Platte-Clay Way
Kearney, Mo. 64060

KE

MID-CONTINENT PUBLIC LIBRARY

3 0000 12364446 4

For our grandchildren . . .
Jennifer Leialoha
Jordan KaLeo onalani
Drew Kaluna
Taylor Malia
. . . and to the children of America and Japan with a hope that you will want to live your lives with peace and tolerance as do the warriors in this book. This wish for a world of peace is even more important on this traumatic and sad day in history.
DN and LN
September 11, 2001

Woodson House Publishing

Pearl Harbor Warriors—the Bugler, the Pilot, the Friendship
Copyright © 2001 Dorinda M. Nicholson, all rights reserved.

Illustrations and Design by Larry Nicholson
Published by Woodson House Publishing P.O. Box 16536 Kansas City, MO 64133
    Phone: 800-555-2693 Email: larry@pearlharborchild.com
    Web Site: www.pearlharborchild.com

Summary
The true story of hatred, fear, prejudice and finally close friendship between an American Marine bugler and his former enemy, a Japanese dive-bomber pilot who had attacked Battleship Row in the bombing of Pearl Harbor.

Nicholson, Dorinda Makanaonalani
    Pearl Harbor Warriors—the Bugler, the Pilot, the Friendship
    by Dorinda Makanaonalani Nicholson; designed/illustrated by Larry Nicholson
    32p., ill., ports.; 23 x 26 cm.
    ISBN 0-931503-05-1
Subjects
    1. [Pearl Harbor (Hawaii), Attack on, 1941 -- Personal narratives]
    2. [USS Arizona Memorial (Hawaii)]
    3. [World War, 1939-1945 -- Hawaii]
    4. [World War, 1939-1945 -- Personal narratives about World War II]
    5. [Friendship]
    6. [Prejudices]
    7. [Hate]
    8. [Ethnic relations-Hawaii]
    9. [Fear]

    940.548/nic -- dc21

Printed by Maywood Willis Printing Company
Printed in the United States of America
First Printing, December 7, 2001

Also by Dorinda Nicholson
"Pearl Harbor Child—a Child's View of
Pearl Harbor from Attack to Peace"
"Pearl Harbor Child Shares Eyewitness
Stories of the Pearl Harbor Attack"
(35 minute Video)

FOREWORD

On a Sunday morning in December of 1941, two young warriors would be swept up in a cyclone of history. They came from different cultures, from different lands, had different military skills and different dreams. One of them grew up in Japan. As a young man, Zenji Abe was educated at the top naval academy in his country, Eta Jima. When he was a child, he dreamed of flight. The vision was realized when he trained to be a naval aviator. That newly acquired skill and his boyhood dream would bring him to Pearl Harbor.

The other warrior had begun life in Massachusetts. His dream was to join the military. He and his high school buddies joined up together, enlisting in the US Marines. Richard Fiske found himself surrounded by his comrades in arms. These new recruits were like Marine Musketeers who now echoed the theme of Dumas "One For All and All For One." Fiske dreamed of adventure and travel. When he enlisted, he joined a proud family committed to military service. His father was in the Navy and his brother was with the Army at Schofield Barracks. Once out of boot camp, he was assigned to a ship stationed in Hawaii. The family was now all together in a place called Pearl Harbor.

On December 7, 1941, that day of death and tragedy, Zenji Abe flew a dive-bomber from the carrier *Akagi* toward his target at Pearl Harbor. Richard Fiske was a Marine bugler on the battleship *West Virginia*. In the desperate two hours of battle, Abe and Fiske unknowingly crossed paths.

The experience of that day had seared into them an impression of war and the failure of peace. In 1991, they first met during a taping of the Today Show. In that moment of prime time morning television, Zenji Abe offered an apology for the attack to members of the Pearl Harbor Survivors and extended his hand in friendship and rapprochement. This was the first step toward reconciliation between Japanese veterans and some of their American counterparts. However, this step was not easy. Not all veterans can do this. The wounds of war don't heal easily, if at all.

Out of the wreckage of World War II emerged these wounded and bloodied veterans. That casual meeting of handshakes and apologies was cemented by their participation in the 50th Anniversary symposium. These two warriors met again and made a private pact to jointly honor the dead of the USS *Arizona*; they had become friends.

I was privileged to witness the beginning of this friendship and watch it mature over the years into brotherhood. Looking back at what transpired between Abe and Fiske brings to mind words of wisdom from my grandfather, who was a civilian survivor of the Pearl Harbor attack: "that bitterness only brings on more bitterness, but, if allowed, time heals all wounds."

This is their incredible story, the story of the healing of those wounds.

Daniel A. Martinez
Historian, National Park Service
USS *Arizona* Memorial

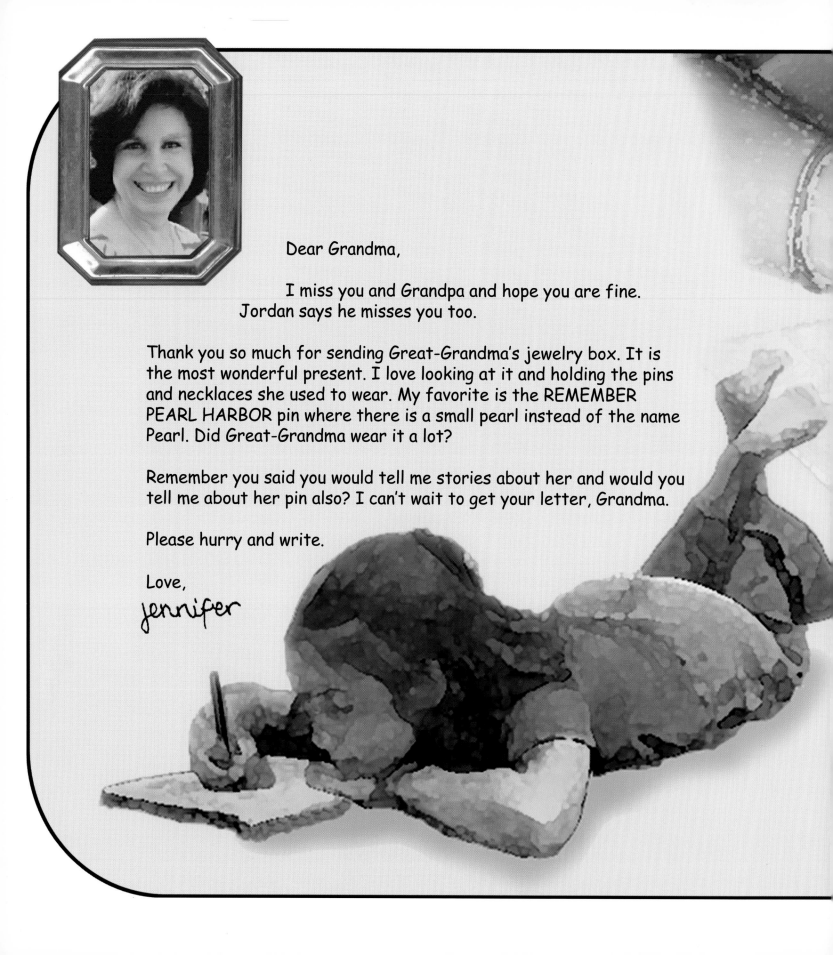

Dear Grandma,

I miss you and Grandpa and hope you are fine.
Jordan says he misses you too.

Thank you so much for sending Great-Grandma's jewelry box. It is
the most wonderful present. I love looking at it and holding the pins
and necklaces she used to wear. My favorite is the REMEMBER
PEARL HARBOR pin where there is a small pearl instead of the name
Pearl. Did Great-Grandma wear it a lot?

Remember you said you would tell me stories about her and would you
tell me about her pin also? I can't wait to get your letter, Grandma.

Please hurry and write.

Love,
Jennifer

My Dear Jennifer,

Yes, there is a story about the REMEMBER PEARL HARBOR pin. It begins way before your daddy was born, and when America was at war with Japan. I was almost your age, when my mom, your great-grandma, proudly wore that pin every time she dressed up. She said it helped her feel patriotic to remember what happened to America at Pearl Harbor on December 7, 1941.

You may have talked about that date at school as the day Japan brought her attack planes by aircraft carriers to bomb Hawaii. America did go to war, and the war cry to always "Remember Pearl Harbor" helped Americans unite in their dislike of the enemy, the Japanese.

Let me tell you how the Japanese hatred began for one 19-year-old American Marine.

Early on a Sunday morning on the 7th of December in 1941, a teenaged Richard Fiske stood erectly on the quarterdeck with his shiny bugle poised in position to sound another "call-to-colors" for his shipmates on the battleship USS West Virginia. Just as he pressed the bugle to his lips and sucked in a deep breath, his eyes caught the brief glint of an airplane as it sped directly toward him. As the plane rushed closer, Dick wondered why the pilot was not pulling up and away from his ship. It was then he saw the torpedo piercing the air and then the water as the mysterious pilot abruptly darted past him. In that brief moment, Fiske had seen America's new enemy. He had stared into the eyes and face of a Japanese torpedo bomber pilot.

Later that morning, he would watch helplessly as his fatally-wounded Captain was gently carried away on a stretcher while still giving commands to his men. Dick says even now, 60 years later, he remembers how sad and difficult that was for him. Moments after their Captain's death, he and his shipmates obeyed orders to abandon ship. Leaping overboard, Dick swam frantically under burning oil to seek refuge on Ford Island.

Long after the air raid, the face of Fiske's attacker haunted him in the daytime and tormented him each night as he struggled to sleep. That phantom face would occupy his nightmares for many years. The hate for the one Japanese pilot became hatred for all Japanese people.

So Jennifer, can you understand why Richard Fiske began to hate the Japanese?
I'm sad to tell you, he was not alone.

So did most Americans.

Lt. Zenji Abe (AH-BAY), the Japanese pilot who eventually would become friends with Fiske, never did hate America or American people. Even in 1945 when the war ended, and he surrendered to U.S. Forces, and was held in a Marine prison camp in Guam for a year and a half, he didn't hate Americans. But, I'm getting way ahead of my story, and you need to know how Fiske and Abe's paths first crossed.

Zenji was a graduate of Japan's Eta Jima Naval Academy, becoming a part of the Imperial Navy. He was highly educated and an extremely skilled pilot.

In the early hours of that December 7th morning, Lt. Zenji Abe, squadron leader, dressed himself in his best flying uniform, the dark khaki-colored one. He solemnly bowed and prayed at the ship's shrine, saying, "I am going now," before climbing into the dive-bomber that would carry him and his navigator from the deck of the aircraft carrier Akagi (AH-KA-GE) to the skies over Pearl Harbor.

Zenji Abe. AKAGI
Pearl Harbor Operation

"I was not excited nor did I feel fear. I was calm and all I cared was to follow orders." It was extremely cloudy that morning and Abe had difficulty seeing land. Then, between masses of white clouds, land and the white waves at Kaneohe Bay came into view. As he rounded the edge of Oahu, he saw the famous landmark of Diamond Head, just a few minutes from his final destination, the U.S. Pacific Fleet at Pearl Harbor.

Abe flew in the second wave of the attack, and so by then the U.S. guns were firing back. "Their aim was frightfully accurate. I was beginning to feel sweat in the back of my neck. When I reached the Harbor, I could see black oily smoke coming up from the ground from the earlier first-wave attack. I dived down to release my bomb, then I gradually pulled up and away to begin my return to the awaiting Akagi."

When Lt. Abe returned to his aircraft carrier, orders were given for the fleet to return immediately to Japan, canceling the third and final wave of bombings over Pearl Harbor. As history would later prove, this retreat was a most fortunate decision for our country.

Jennifer, there were several reasons for the retreat decision: the surprise advantage was gone; the Americans would be more prepared to fight back; it was still unknown where America's aircraft carriers were, and Japan couldn't chance losing theirs. Finally, Japan's attempt to forewarn America that peace talks were over between our countries arrived in Washington, D.C. after the attack had already begun! This caused Japan to lose face and honor, because they had attacked without giving warning.

The next day, President Roosevelt asked Congress to declare war on Japan. American Marine Fiske and Japanese Lt. Abe were now enemy warriors from opposite sides of the world.

When, if ever, would their paths cross again?

After Lt. Abe returned on the *Akagi* to Japan, he served in the South Pacific and on other aircraft carriers before becoming a flight instructor and commanding officer. On one of his flights he crash-landed in the Marianas Islands and had to survive living in the jungle for a year. After Japan surrendered to America, he became our prisoner for 15 months in a United States Marine Corps camp in Guam. When released, he returned home to Japan.

Even though Fiske's ship, the USS *West Virginia*, was sunk by nine torpedoes and two bombs, it was raised, repaired and able to fight again. Fiske stayed on board until January 1944 when he was transferred to the 5th Marine Division. He was at Iwo Jima for the landing and the bloody battle that lasted 34 days. He said it was horrible, bodies everywhere; 7,000 marines and 20,000 Japanese died.

While our U.S. military forces were on the war front defending America, we on the home front wanted to do our share to help our "troops." Our family helped by planting a victory garden (how I hated to pull the weeds), collecting metal to recycle into ammunition, and would you believe it, I also became a "show girl!"

Your grandma helped entertain the troops stationed in Hawaii by being in USO shows. I'm the littlest dancer on the left and Great-Grandma Momi, our teacher, is on the far right. Did I ever tell you her nickname Momi means pearl for Pearl Harbor? The name of her hula studio was Hale Momi (HA-LAY MO-MEE, House of Pearl.) The hula girls of Hale Momi felt very patriotic when smiling and performing our wartime show "Pearl City Frolic."

I've also sent you my wartime stamp book. Do you see where I still have some 25 cent stamps in it? I went without milk at school so I could buy the stamps to fill the book to get a war bond. That way, little kids like your grandma could help loan money to America to fight a very expensive war.

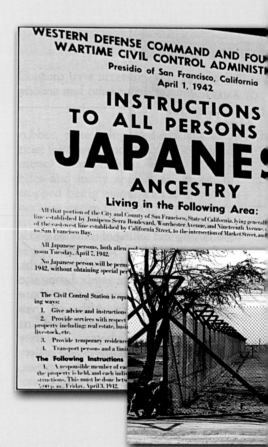

I'm the girl behind the gas mask with my little brother. Everyone in Hawaii had to have one and we even had practice drills at school. When the wail of air raid sirens sounded, we were to scurry in an orderly manner to the air raid shelter while pulling the musty-smelling masks over our faces.

The role of women changed dramatically and quickly during this time when most of the men were away at war. Women rolled up their sleeves and said we can take care of the home front. Many went to work in factories building planes and tanks. We called "her", Rosie the Riveter.

The saddest part of American home front history is what happened out of fear and distrust of Americans of Japanese ancestry, even though most were loyal United States citizens. Remember my writing how Americans hated the Japanese? Because of hate and prejudice, thousands upon thousands of Japanese were forced to abandon their homes to live in barren, barbed-wire internment camps.

It was even sadder for the Japanese people in their homeland of Japan.

In Japan, Lt. Abe's people suffered greatly during the war. There were severe food shortages, and people were always hungry. Their home front was not safe, nor thousands of miles away from the war front, as in the United States.

Our country frequently sent airplanes to bomb their country, destroying huge cities and many lives. Finally, America dropped the deadly atomic bomb on August 6, 1945. Over one hundred thousand people were killed. Thousands of other victims would suffer infections, disfigurement, and constant pain for many years afterward. Less than 10 days later, Japan surrendered. Grimly, finally, the war ended.

on the _____ SECOND _____ day of _____ SEPTEMBER _____, 1945.

重光葵

By Command and in behalf of the Emperor of Japan
and the Japanese Government.

梅津美治郎

By Command and in behalf of the Japanese
Imperial General Headquarters.

Accepted at _____ TOKYO BAY, JAPAN _____ at _____ 0903 I _____
on the _____ SECOND _____ day of _____ SEPTEMBER _____, 1945,
for the United States, Republic of China, United Kingdom and the
Union of Soviet Socialist Republics, and in the interests of the other
United Nations at war with Japan.

Douglas MacArthur
Supreme Commander for the Allied Powers.

C.W. Nimitz
United States Representative

徐永昌
Republic of China Representative

Bruce Fraser
United Kingdom Representative

Kuzma Derevyanko
Union of Soviet Socialist Republics
Representative

Wasn't that a sad ending to the war, Jen?

With Japan agreeing to surrender, a formal peace treaty was signed in Tokyo Bay on September 2, 1945. The ceremony took place on a huge U.S. battleship numbered 63 and named "USS Missouri." As the leaders of our countries signed the official document, hundreds of American airplanes circled cautiously overhead.

Many other ships were also in the harbor to witness the solemn occasion. However, I think you would enjoy knowing that one of them was Fiske's former battleship, the salvaged and repaired USS West Virginia.

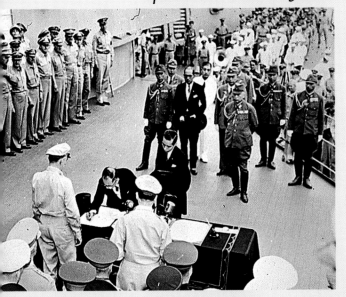

Although it was a joyous day for Americans, it was a sad time for Lt. Abe and his family. He was not going home but would become a prisoner of war, enduring a 15-month sentence. When he was released in 1946, he went home to the bombed-out city of Tokyo. Eventually he would retire from the Navy and return to private life, devoting his energy to rebuilding his country and being with his family.

Sgt. Fiske returned home and then re-enlisted in the newly formed Air Force, serving first in Korea and later in Vietnam. Eventually, he returned to the private life of an ordinary civilian.

Well my dear Jen, that's the end of the war and the end of the story of your great-grandma's Remember Pearl Harbor pin. After the war ended, my mom must have dropped it into a deep corner of her jewelry box. I think it's been waiting there for you to find it and hear its story.

With aloha,

Grandma

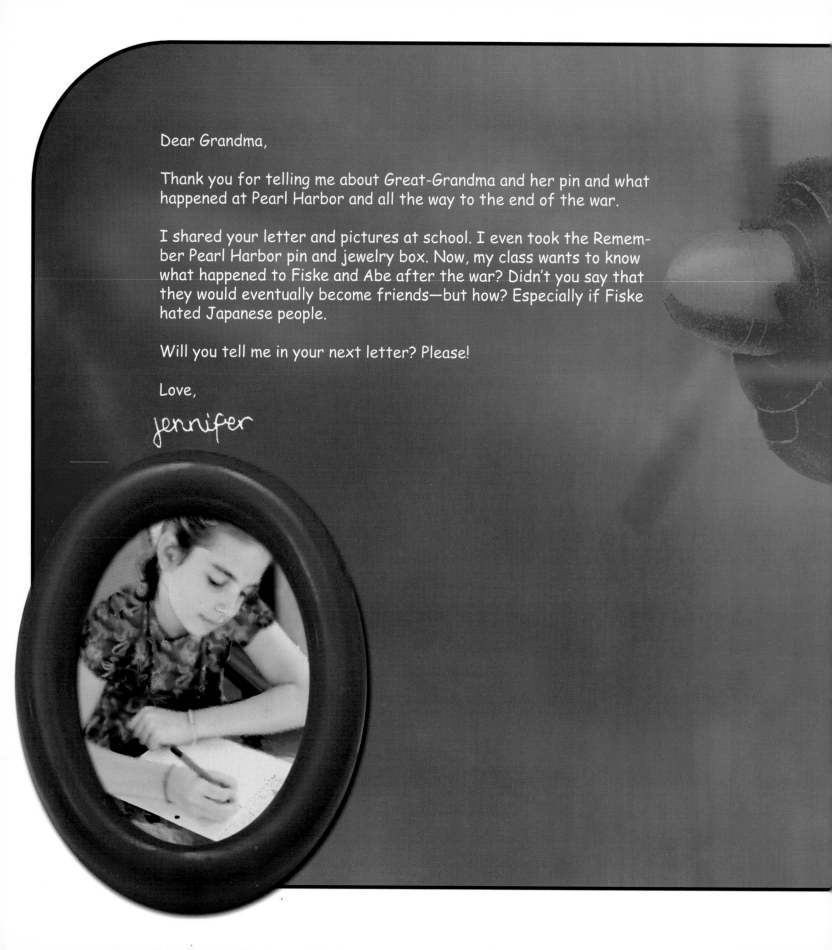

Dear Grandma,

Thank you for telling me about Great-Grandma and her pin and what happened at Pearl Harbor and all the way to the end of the war.

I shared your letter and pictures at school. I even took the Remember Pearl Harbor pin and jewelry box. Now, my class wants to know what happened to Fiske and Abe after the war? Didn't you say that they would eventually become friends—but how? Especially if Fiske hated Japanese people.

Will you tell me in your next letter? Please!

Love,

jennifer

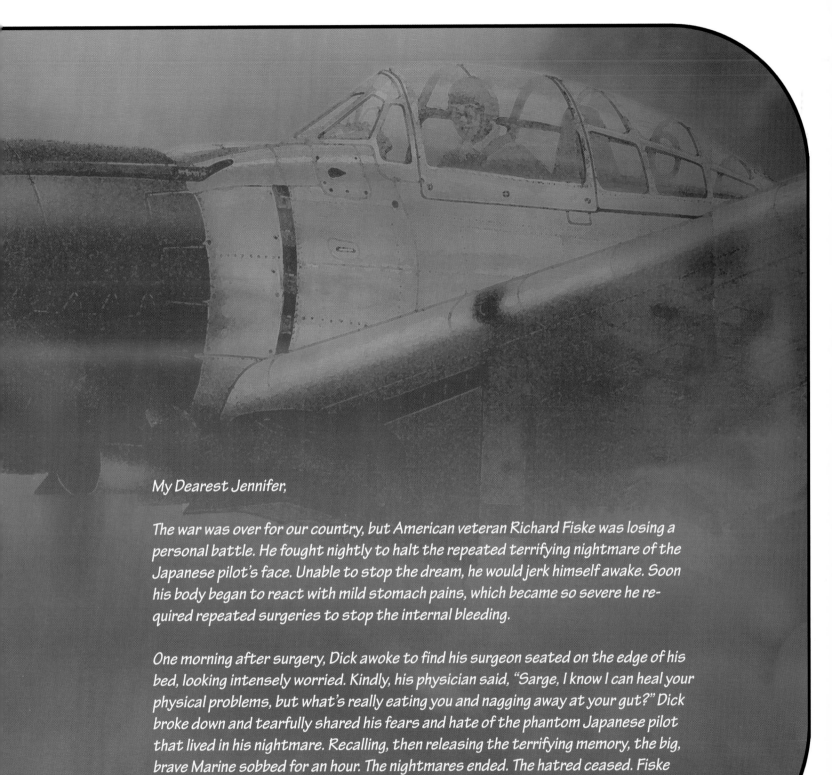

My Dearest Jennifer,

The war was over for our country, but American veteran Richard Fiske was losing a personal battle. He fought nightly to halt the repeated terrifying nightmare of the Japanese pilot's face. Unable to stop the dream, he would jerk himself awake. Soon his body began to react with mild stomach pains, which became so severe he required repeated surgeries to stop the internal bleeding.

One morning after surgery, Dick awoke to find his surgeon seated on the edge of his bed, looking intensely worried. Kindly, his physician said, "Sarge, I know I can heal your physical problems, but what's really eating you and nagging away at your gut?" Dick broke down and tearfully shared his fears and hate of the phantom Japanese pilot that lived in his nightmare. Recalling, then releasing the terrifying memory, the big, brave Marine sobbed for an hour. The nightmares ended. The hatred ceased. Fiske said, "That was the day my heart grew a lot bigger."

Fiske didn't want to hate anymore. To completely let go of old painful memories, he knew he needed to share his story.

This former Marine, now armed with only a scrapbook of memories and a big warm smile, began to share his story while chatting with visitors as a National Park Service volunteer at the USS Arizona Memorial. As he continued to serve as one of the Park's goodwill ambassadors, he met some former Japanese pilots who were visiting Hawaii.

One of them spoke English and so Fiske said, "Wouldn't it be great if we could get the guys who bombed Pearl Harbor together with our American veterans?" A Japanese newspaper picked up the story and printed it saying that American veterans were putting out their hands in friendship.

ソンさん（左）、フィスクさん（右）とバージリオさん

真珠湾攻撃50周年

In Tokyo, Zenji Abe was encouraged by the photo story and was hopeful that it might be possible to begin a reconciliation between American and Japanese veterans. So when he received an invitation to attend a meeting of one of the Pearl Harbor Survivors' Association chapters, he readily accepted. Abruptly, the invitation was withdrawn. Other American veterans had protested, saying Japan must first apologize, and they threatened to walk out of any meetings the Japanese attended. Jen, I remember reading about the controversy in the newspapers. It seemed our country had gone back to hating and using names like "Jap" again.

Meanwhile, the Japanese veterans immediately canceled all travel plans, but not all plans for reconciliation. Abe and a group of Japanese veterans wanting friendship, remembered the photo story of the Americans extending a hand of welcome. Encouraged by the photo of the three smiling Americans, a small group of veterans traveled to Pearl Harbor to attend the 50th Anniversary Syposium in December of 1991. The Symposium ended with a dramatic and unplanned show of goodwill. The next spring, another group of Japanese veterans returned to Pearl Harbor. This time, these former enemies came with their hands extended in friendship.

After returning to Japan, Abe felt encouraged about future reconciliations, but discouraged about feelings of hate that still existed between many American and Japanese people. He wondered what he could personally do to help erase some of the hate. About then, Fiske sent a letter to Abe saying, "Abe-san, yesterday's enemy is today's friend. I don't hate Japanese anymore, please come to Hawaii. We will have dinner, talk, hug, and cry together."

Here's the picture of Fiske and Abe meeting in Hawaii at the beginning of their special relationship. It had been fifty years since their paths first crossed in Pearl Harbor; the young Japanese dive-bomber pilot and the even-younger Marine bugler. Now, no longer young, they both felt an urgency to heal old war wounds and dissolve old hatreds.

Even though language barriers made casual conversation difficult, both men felt a deep bond of friendship develop between them. Abe could feel Fiske's warm, friendly spirit. For the two of them, yesterday's enemy was indeed today's friend.

These two friends felt passionately about helping to erase old hatreds . Abe had a plan. Of course, he would need Fiske's help.

Just before Abe was to return to Japan, he asked Richard for a favor. "Richard-san," he said, "I want to give you some money. Would you please use it to buy two red roses each month, one for you, and the other for me? Then would you take the roses out to the Arizona Memorial and play Taps on your bugle? This is my way to say, 'I'm sorry.'" Fiske agreed, saying, "I too am sorry. War is hell. It will be an honor to do this in memory of all those who died. I will make a vow to go each month for both of us as long as I possibly can."

Fiske's commitment began in May of 1992. The ceremony is a simple one. On the last Sunday afternoon of each month, the tall, white-mustached Richard Fiske steps off a boat and onto the gleaming white *Arizona* Memorial. In one hand, he holds two ruby red roses; in the other, his shiny bright bugle. Silently, he gently carries the roses to the back of the memorial, reverently places them at the base of the light gray wall deeply carved with names of the men killed in the bombing of the USS *Arizona*.

Then, Fiske steps back, turns, and faces the visitors fortunate to be there as witnesses to the healing ceremony created by two former enemies. Since there is no formal program or announcement, he asks the audience to honor the memory of those who have died for their country, and then sends a wish for a future of peace and friendship.

Lifting his bugle, he presses the mouthpiece against his lips, just as he did on a long-ago December 7th morning. This time, he will not be interrupted by war and nightmares. This time, nothing will hold back the mournful sound of Taps as it fills the memorial. Nothing will stop the emotions raised by those familiar, echoing notes. And when the last note fades away, Fiske knows that once again, he has kept the promise made in friendship to his Japanese warrior friend, Zenji Abe.

Jennifer, isn't that a beautiful ceremony? I'm so glad you wanted to know their friendship story. Now, watch your mailbox—you have a surprise coming. I'll write you in a few days to see what you think.

Love,

Grandma

Honolulu, Hawaii
September 24, 2001

Dear Jennifer,

Your grandma asked me to tell you about my special friendship with my former enemy, Zenji Abe. I'm always happy to do so, because I want people to understand that we don't have to have war. We can become friends with our so-called adversaries.

I want young kids like you to understand that war is hell.

My main mission in life is to get kids to understand that it's not glorified like you see on TV. That's not the real war, it's just for shock purposes or an attempt to entertain. In real war, you are maimed and killed. I remember when we landed in Iwo Jima, about the fifth or sixth assault wave. When I hit the beach there were bodies all over the place. It was horrible. Kids today think they're invincible, but they're not.

People sometimes call us heroes. We're not. The real heroes are the women, the mothers, the wives, the grandmothers, the sisters, and the sweethearts. They were the ones who kept that link between the home front and us in the field. That's so important, because it gave us the sense of belonging to someone and something. Without that, we're all alone, and that's a terrible feeling. We all need to belong to something and someone.

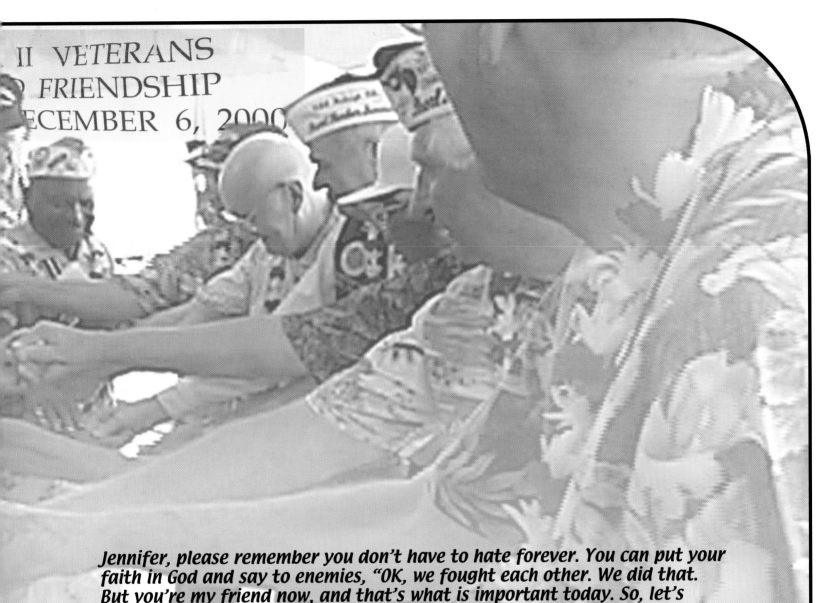

II VETERANS
FRIENDSHIP
ECEMBER 6, 2000

Jennifer, please remember you don't have to hate forever. You can put your faith in God and say to enemies, "OK, we fought each other. We did that. But you're my friend now, and that's what is important today. So, let's build on that."

There are three words I want you to always remember: friendship, love and truth. You live by them, and this world will be a better and safer place.

Your friend,

Richard Fiske
USS West Virginia

Richard Fiske
USS West Virginia

Koganei, Japan
September 23, 2001

Dear Jennifer,

I am an old man now—85 years old. Sixty years
ago, I was a young dive-bomber pilot in the air
raid on Pearl Harbor. America and Japan went to
war for four years, but now, United States and
Japan are friendly countries.

I have come to like Americans very much as your
people are cheerful, openhearted, and generous.
I have many American friends, but Mr. Fiske is
a most special friend in my heart. Even though
we did not shake hands until long after the war
ended, I believe our friendship was predestined,
as we share a special connection in our lives
because our paths first crossed in Pearl Harbor
on December 7, 1941.

Japan was a poor country in 1941. The Japanese
people were suffering and trying to solve this
problem, and so our two countries went to war.
My life then was to defend and help my country.
Now my life is devoted to my family, rebuilding
my country, repairing friendships with former
enemies, and writing a book to educate Japanese
people about Pearl Harbor and the importance of
the attack in world history.

I think it is great that you are asking your
grandmother to help you understand history.
Children can learn from the mistakes of the
past and maybe teach their countries how to
spread peace all over the world. There are many
countries in our small mother earth. We need to
recognize each does have its own history, cul-
ture, and customs. It is most important we work
together to understand each other.

Love,

Zenji Abe

Zenji Abe